AF504385

GIGS *the* ROBOT · BUNNY

By: Melanie Kallai
Illustrations: Joyce Knarr

Book Cover and Layout by Joel Kivett / www.joelkivett.com

Illustrations by Joyce Knarr

First edition 2024

For my sweet son, Leo,
who gave me the idea
for Gigs in the first place.

Gigs the robot bunny felt all alone,
for he lived in a box on a shelf.
It was hardly a place to call home, you see,
because Gigs was all by himself.

Children passed him day after day
for a shinier, fancier friend.
One day, a truck drove up to the store—
his shelf life had come to an end.

YIKE!
MONSTER
WOW!
PLANETS!
LOOK
SEE!!
GIGS
Robot Bunny Robot Bunny
Robot Bunny Robot Bunny
* GIGS
ON SALE!
SUPER
PLASMA
EARTH GLOBE
FUN!
FUN
NOW!!
YOU BUILD!
FUTURE CITY!!

I
HAUL

He was taken out back in a garbage bin
feeling broken and down on his luck.
But as he closed his eyes for good
his box burst open, he fell off the truck.

So off he went with his hopes sky-high
in search of his place in the world.
He hopped and hopped to a farm nearby
where animals frolicked and twirled.

"A perfect home, so open and green,"
Gigs said as he took in the sight.
"Now, who wants to be my very first friend?"
he asked, and looked left and right.

Some had feathers, and others had wool.
There were round and furry ones, too.
Some were tall, and one jumped in the air.
Some were quacky, and "Hey, who are you?"

He liked how they lived there, all kinds and all shapes-
a robot could learn to chew straw.
"I'll stay here forever," Gigs said and spun 'round,
and a smile cracked his cold metal jaw.

The animals looked from their pastures and pens
at the strange little bundle of bolts.
But there was no laughter, and there were no grins
from the pigs or the calf or the colts.

" You're lucky, dear cows, to have pigs nearby,
and horses and little goats, too.
It must be a treasure to play together;
I want to be just like you."

" It's better to stay with our own kind;
we are very different, you see."
" Now leave us to graze," a spotted cow said.
" This is the way it must be."

Outside of the barn were geese and goats,
but they glared when Gigs came near.
They worried that Gigs might take their food,
so they chased him away out of fear.

"You don't understand me. I don't drink or eat.
All I want is a friend so I can be complete."

Unsure of the robot that came from town,
the chickens stopped pecking their corn.
He whirred and flashed while he hopped in the barn
to see that a lamb had been born.

G

G

"I've never seen a new baby before.
Do you know what her name will be?"
"Who cares," bocked the chickens.
"She'll grow to a sheep.
There is nothing momentous to see."

Gigs wondered about the chicken's response
as he watched Mama Sheep love her lamb,
and could not comprehend the animals there,
as he hopped by a very proud ram.

Two little foals whinnied and pranced close by.
Surely, they wanted to play.
The chicks looked eager to greet them,
but the grown horses whisked them away.

"We do not play with the barnyard fowl.
  That's not the way of the horse."
"Why not?" asked a very curious Gigs.
"Because they have feathers, of course!"

He thought about what the animals said
and watched them for hours that day.
And yes, they did some things differently;
they all had their own unique way.

But mostly, Gigs thought they were quite alike.
He computed that from the start.
They lived side by side on a beautiful farm
and yet they still lived apart.

Gigs looked down at his cold metal arms,
as the smile fell away from his face.
"I am the different one," he said,
"in need of a welcoming place.

I don't have warm feathers or fur.
I'm only metal and lights.
But, to live with you here in the barn and the fields,
would fill me with endless delights.

You could be a marvelous family
if you'd only give it a try.
You are warm and soft and wonderful.
You laugh, and you love, and you cry."

The animals stopped and listened to Gigs.
His words weren't crazy at all.
But how could this bunny know such things?
He was little more than a doll.

Yet he stood there and saw
what the others could not—
a thought so very big
from a little robot.

The animals stared but did not say a word,
for they were deep in thought.
Gigs waited and gave one last flickering beep.
But a friend here? He had not.

Gigs turned around and hopped away.
His tiny, cold heart was broken that day.

But the animals heard every word that he said,
that robot bunny named Gigs.
They realized how special their little farm was,
the horses and chickens and pigs.

The cows made friends with the goats and the geese,
and the horses and sheep shared the hay.
The chickens and pigs met the newborn lamb,
but something else happened that day.

G

As Gigs came to the edge of the farm,
feeling friendless and still all alone,
a chorus of voices urged him back
in a kind, inviting tone.

"Stay with us, Gigs," the animals begged.
"There's plenty of land here to roam.
You've shown us that we are a family,
and we want you to call our farm home."

the END

Melanie Kallai grew up in the eccentric little town of Gibsonton, Florida, a place from which she frequently draws story inspiration. She holds a diploma in Advanced Fiction Writing and Screenwriting from the University of Cambridge and a B.A. in Evolutionary Biology and Ecology from the University of Colorado. Her flash fiction has been published by The Dillydoun Review and Reservoir Road, and her memoir, What We Keep, was published in the 2020 Colorado Book Award-winning anthology, Rise: An Anthology of Change. She lives in Colorado with her husband and son.

Joyce Knarr (pronounce the K), born in St. Petersburg, Florida, and raised in Sarasota, has spent her adult life in the Tampa Bay Area. A portrait artist as well as designer, her first illustrations were published in 2002. Her reputation as an artist who conveys feelings and emotions is evident in all of her work and variety of mediums. Joyce is the mother of two daughters, three granddaughters, and soon-to-be great-grandmother of another girl!

GIGS
the
ROBOT · BUNNY